MW01089505

TO: ROZ

I'm honored to bring
back your inspiration :)

♡

'07

:)

young skin
Wise Mind
OLD SOUL

By

Amanda Diva Seales

authorHOUSE

1663 LIBERTY DRIVE, SUITE 200
BLOOMINGTON, INDIANA 47403
(800) 839-8640
www.authorhouse.com

© 2005 Amanda Diva Seales
All Rights Reserved.

No part of this book may be reproduced, stored in a retrieval system, or transmitted by any means without the written permission of the author.

First published by AuthorHouse 03/30/05

ISBN: 1-4184-5683-7 (e)
ISBN: 1-4184-3689-5 (sc)

Library of Congress Control Number: 2004091422

Printed in the United States of America
Bloomington, Indiana

This book is printed on acid-free paper.

I welcome ya'll to take a lyrical journey through this, my first collection of poems. *Young Skin/ Wise Mind/ Old Soul*, is about growth and its continuous presence in the lives of all artists. We all have to start somewhere and these poems are my beginning. Thanks for being here to see it. ~Deev

Table of Contents

Amanda was a very *intense* child.- Nettie

young skin

Oreo

I used to be told I sounded white because I was easily understood

My speech didn't hold the rhythm of the hood

An oreo/ with Black on the outside and white in the middle

The kids said I didn't sound like my race not even a little

So I wasn't even a perpetrator because that's just who I was

A black girl/ with white talk/ who didn't ride the bus

So that meant I was rich

And I thought I was "all that"

Been threatened many a time to get bashed and wacked

Even once to be thrown through a window

So/ I had to let them know

I have no dough

I'm not rich

I'm not all that

I'm not white on the inside

My soul just like yours is black

But until I could quote TuPac

And shake my ass

Until I could use "aight" in my everyday speech

And wasn't afraid to skip class

My speech was foreign to my African American peers ears

Until I could hold the rhythm of the streets in my hips and tongue

My presence of off-blackness was met with blank stares that on to
me they flung

It stung

And only when I met the standard set by BET and the local hip-
hop and r&b station

Did I gain residence in the hip-hop nation

I've been living here comfortably as a resident since the eleventh
grade

As a person with skin of a darker shade than peach

Funny/ for a time I thought there was a pinnacle of blackness I
had to reach

Just to fill out my skin's melanin

Now I realize that it's not that I wasn't black until I was approved
of by my peers

They couldn't pass me the baton

I've been in this race for 19 years

I Hate

This is one of my earlier pieces, when I began to find my voice as a poet. It is rather harsh, but it is a part my evolution.

They say that HATE is a strong word

Well/ i use it daily

Because i HATE/ i HATE/ i HATE

That people try to dull my brilliance by calling me crazy

Or take my patience for my life's planning as being lazy

How the hell/ can hearing that continuously *not* phase me

i HATE that it does

i HATE/ i HATE/ i HATE that it does

i HATE that i'm not the brick wall everyone believes me to be

i HATE that i'm not the rubber band bouncing off any disrupting
   thoughts to my continuous developing of me

i HATE that i'm not the famous star yet that for every year of my
   life has been predicted like it was the weather

i HATE that right now it's like i'm hanging from a string of life
   like i was a ball and the string its tether

i HATE that now i'm heavy like a rock

Remember when i used to be light as a feather

The strength of the word HATE isn't easy to measure

For some it's the weight of steel

For me its scale is tempered by how i feel

i HATE that it seems like nobody anymore acts real

i'm for real when i say i HATE

Cause

i don't not care

i don't just dislike

i don't think "that's not fair"

i don't just say "they trife"

Cause i HATE that life ain't fair

And i HATE that shit gets trife

But in the end i cry and get over it cause it doesn't make sense to
    just hate LIFE

Journey from the Dark Side

(*twilight zone music*)

Tonight I will take you to a place many have experienced, but few have told the tale. A place where exists a silent constrictor. Preventing the minds of many of all different shades of brown to open, it feasts on ignorance and thrives on division. The beast I speak of is intra-racial racism. Tonight folks, I will take you on a journey from the darker side of the Black race. Welcome to...THE LIGHT SKINNED ZONE.

I've never been called a spook

Porch monkey or picaninny

But I have been called a light skinned kinky haired bitch who
  think she pretty

Labeled high-sadiddy for my "high yellow" skin

A brotha even addressed me as light/ bright/ and almost white
  one night when I was walkin through Harlem

So often I hear about racism

Whether it's the White Man

The Jewish lady in my building

Or someone blamin the system

And though those scenarios are in a constant existence

It's within the microcosm of the Black community where I've been
  the brunt of intraracial obscenity

My chocolate/ ebony/ and mahogany sistas

They say the blacker the berry the sweeter the juice

But my lack of melanin don't make mine any less richer than
yours

My core is a deep hue like the blackness of the blues

It knows rivers/ built pyramids/ and came to this country on slave
ships

Not no pleasure cruise

For those of you who think there's no link

Between dark skin and mine

Go back to the gallows and you'll find us linked shackle to shackle
standin in line

Or chain to chain working on the railroad grind

Realign your senses and take a ride

Journey from the dark side

To where I reside

A lioness with a caramel colored hide

I may not come from your hood

But I know about your block

My ancestors may have been in the house

While yours were in the fields

But they all stood on the auction block

Many are quick to spit that unity shit

But when it comes down to it

Think soul is determined by how God painted the epidermis
protecting your limbs

Not what's within

To some my skin is a blessing

To others it's a blatant confessing

That white blood is filtered throughout our race

And anyone displaying that is worth dispossessing

Well I will not be acquiescing to either of those opinions

Serving as one of society's standards minions

This is my kingdom

I rule over this dominion

But it doesn't matter how many times I say that I'm a Queen

To many my skin just ain't dark enough for the crown to be seen

I am light...on my feet

Cause I'm not weighted down with bullshit

I am bright

Cause my brain is lit with electrodes and neurons flowing with the
currents of the intelligent

And I am almost white...house eligible

Only 15 more years

Till I can reside over this nation

The first Black female president

Me and Washington's portraits will hang adjacent

I was born by the river

So I say it loud

I'm Black and I'm proud

Rebellin against conforming like a Mau Mau

All of ya'll who wonder how or why

I raise my fist so high

Journey from the dark side

And see the lighter side of the other side of the racial divide

I check the box that says Black or African-American

I come from children pickin cotton below the Mason-Dixon

My people were sovereign to the Caribbean

Before Columbus called them West Indian

So to anyone believing

That Blackness is determined by one's abundance of melanin

Answer this question

Black is defined as the absence of color

We're a brown people

So in actuality where do any of us really fit in

This is the first poem I ever wrote. EVERRRRR! It came about during my Dramatic Structure class in my first semester at SUNY Purchase back in 1999. It's comedy, ain't nothing like seeing growth on paper! I've become a New Yorker, no doubt, but I'll never forget where I'm from. JEAH!

The Dirty South

I form words in my mouth representing the Dirty South

Where the sun hits hard

All day playing cards and ball

Niggas at the beach sippin on Sysco

Juvenile playin every mile in the Monte Carlo

Got no dough

But we'll still grow though

Can't stop us just cause we below the Mason Dixon

We be fixin collard greens and southern fried chicken

Sweat be drippin all day and afternoon

Dancin outside Aquemini echoes through palm trees

And hookers on OBT are lit by the reflection of the moon

Hot dogs at 7-Eleven at 12 at night

When you leave the club there's always gonna be a fight

New Balance and Saucony takin over all areas

It's hysteria

Do you have the criteria to call yourself a Dirty Southern

Where golds and tatts represent how you govern your community

Where niggas are too strong to ask for immunity

They're dirty dirty cause They're wilin

Even stylin

Stepping in and out of Everglades

While up north niggas is too busy

Look for a slit of shade

Meltin through your Enyce/ Phatfarm/ and Mecca

When down south them niggas bustin in some jeans and wife
   beater

While you fantasize about Linden and the Boogie down

The A/ the D/ the F/ Queens and Uptown

I'm chillin like a villain

Takin rides with no conditionin/ air that is

Just wind through four windows whistling

Rims spinnin quick

Suckin on a lic-a-stic

Not a dirty foot or a trick

Just a southern booty chick

Blarin Fiend/ Silkk/ and Mystical

Them niggas from No Limit

I got the boom in my trunk

Proceeded by that tick tick

Cause southern girls like me

Love that music that makes you go ballistic

BLING BLING

Cell phones and beepers ring ring

Through river snaked states

Where the Black man's life

Was once held by the white man's fate

See we're sittin on Confederate residue

Lookin at the cotton fields with a different view

Black and Milds changing up the color and the hue

I do what I do and stay true to that crew

That represents the southeast region

We a legion of niggas pimpin lacks

With dats and spoilers on the back

Talkin that they "Fo real"

"Rowdy Rowdy"

And "Bout it Bout it"

See them southern boys swear they hot

Got that game

Sportin gold chains and tatts

Displayin they nicknames like "Pooh"/ "Kool-Aid"/ "Mike Mike"/ "Red"/ and "Pookie"

Spittin out to the ladies, "Pssst" and "Aaaah, sookie sookie"

We a different breed of cats

With a culture all our own

From VA/ Tennessee/ Mississippi/ Bama

Georgia/ Texas/ Arkansas/ Louisiana

Florida/ Kentucky/ West Virginia

We got that North and that South Carolina

Or as they call it/ Kakalacka

Red beans and rice assembled on my plate

As I sit and concentrate

On how to correlate

The north to the south

The Hot Boys to the Ruff Ryders

In the south/ colors don't me no harm to me

My dawgs are soldiers rollin with an army

We ain't unlawful

It's got to be impossible

For even you Yankees not to join in as we "Back that ass up"

Cause getting krunk is ensuing

We "Hoody-hooin" that's how we see it

Cause I'm from the DIRTY SOUTH nigga

Can you really feel it

Thug Lessons

Thug lessons I'm learning summer I was turning 19

Through suburban eyes/ these culturized Brooklyn streets is seen

Brown bodies/ island accents/ weaves glistening with Afro sheen

Bootleg seller/ makin money green

Beans and rice/ at the corner store for a small price

Scurrying through the 24 hour market like mice

City infested like lice/ with less than what we really deserve

A dollar van makes a swerve as an expedition swings around the
     curve

Nervous mothers clutchin little hands/ already knowin fists to the
     dome

I live four stoops down from a foster home

These kids is stealin bread

Twists/ cornrows/ and locks/ in they little heads

Playin with blades like they was marbles

Marvel at how horrible this place ain't to visit but it would be to be
     stuck

Luck took the train uptown

The D left you a sitting duck

Gum speckled sidewalks reminding me of chicken pox

Crip niggas in front of Kennedy's at 2 a.m. sellin rocks

Church and Flatbush no cushion

but cement

I buy my dollar double A batteries

So this woman can pay her rent

Keep It Together

~March 16, 2002

Sometimes I have to take a moment

Stop and breathe

Cause everyday everybody deals with their own struggle

But sometimes it feels like yours is gonna knock you to your knees

So I breathe

And whisper to myself

Keep it together

Keep it together

This too shall pass

Things will get better

But how do you keep it together

When even in the light of coming blessings

You still feel clouded by the weather

"No one could've seen it comin"

"She's in a better place"

"Just be happy that you're healthy"

"He's not the one for you"

"All ease your mind for a minute"

But then you're back in it

Tryin to find the answers to questions

You don't even know how to ask

Enlightenment is not an easy task

How do you

Keep it together

Keep it together

When the one you trusted in

Comes to you all of a sudden

To say he realized that it wasn't love he was in

And that though yesterday he was callin you his wife

Today it's, "can't you just understand and be my friend

Cause I don't want to lose you

And I respect you so I won't disconnect you"

I feel the scream from my throat creepin

But I hold it in

Don't want to wil' out

Cause what's it worth in the end

Walk around with my chin up

Though inside I'm cryin

Tryin to get it through my head

What everybody's sayin

"He's not the one for you Amanda

So fuck him!"

But I'm stuck in a place of logic entrapped with emotion

The future I'm not knowin

But time's steady flowin so I

Keep it together

Keep it together

Through the stormy weather

Cause I'm held by a tether of reality

To seeing everything around me with clarity

But how do you see

When you're in a mist of criticism

Not even by the ones who hold the numbers

But by your own mental system

Your mind can become your own prison

If you let it lock you in

To a place of appealing/ appeasing/ and agreeing

Thinking

Will they feel it

Hope he liked it

She was clappin

Yo they hyped it

But more importantly

Is when it's just you and the mic

Shinin in your own light

Are you happy with yourself

And was it worth the fight

"Be happy you have your health"

My mom tells me

When frustration sets in

And I agree cause as long as my heart's beatin

I can try again

But when I'm down and trudging through the mud

Not knowin my destination

I just keep sayin

Keep it together

Keep it together

But it's hard to be tough like leather

When life gets beneath your skin

Got people around me suddenly dyin

Pickin up the phone

To somber tones of a mother holdin her pain in

Tellin me her daughter died at 7:30am yesterday morning

My friend who I had just spoke to that weekend

Tellin me about her job and her new apartment

Gone in a flash

Meningitis in the brain

24 hours of pain

Now she's gone and I'll never see her again

Keep it together

Shit/ I'm fightin from burstin at the seams

People are not always as together as they seem

One that I thought I knew

And deemed one of the most talented emcees

Possessing style/ skill/ and intelligentsia

Was diagnosed two weeks ago with Paranoid Schizophrenia

And everyone is up in arms

Confused and sayin

"No one could've seen this comin Amanda"

But I saw the signs

I just didn't know what they were relayin

And now every morning/ on the train/ at work/ on stage/ all day

I'm prayin

Sayin

Keep it together

Keep it together

When I want to throw a chair through the window

Punch a hole in the wall

Scream and yell and run down the hall

Hopin soon I'll again see the day

Whey my mind was simply inclined to rhyme

And I smiled content and happy

But then I see

I need these times to write these rhymes

To climb to higher elevations/ I

Keep it together

Keep it together

Because I have to be patient

And though I cease the moment

I know when the moment ain't

Never a victim to time

I'm watchin my clock

Lookin for signs/ I

Keep it together

Keep it together

Cause that's what I simply have to do

To survive in this world

Wait for the scroll to unfurl

And to myself/ my art/ and my loved ones

Always be true

As I Await my Flight

Felt I could weather any storm

But I've got a cloudy perception

My recollection remembers so many promises now lost to the
   wind

I wrote them in stone

But you scripted them

      in erasable pen

            almost permanent

But removable when needed

I stand defeated

Face to face with my match

One who caught my heart

I was glad to give it

Then left it   in left field

When he no longer needed it

I've got corrective lenses

But still can't see straight

Blinded by love before

Now in a mist of hate

Groping through the bullshit

Searchin for my cardiac

I want in back

Fully intact

No strings attached

Lacking any hint of a dent

Or a breath of a scratch

But you're still holding it

Cause this is mind over matter

Can't free it from your possession

Till in my mind you no longer matter

I'm still cryin

Hatin your lying

Still tearin up in public places

Wiping tears off my face its

An unfamiliar place this

Broken heart hell

I find myself in

Keep

                                 out

                    crawl

            to

tryin

but I fall right back in.

For You in Your Absence

~for DJB

I wrote this in the absence of your presence

To calm my nerves

To clear my mind

To gain control

To ease my load

To talk to you through words

Cause unlike touch they don't dissolve with distance

They marinate with time

So I rhyme

To the rhythm of my love for you

Kinda like the mix between a Roots beat and an Al Green groove

I feel you with my eyes closed

Getting glimpses of innervisions like Stevie

My daydreams have taken on a new identity

They are now reflections of the reality of you and me

I take them in

Throughout the day

And they

Like the rays of radiation

To carcinogens

Dissipate any hint of negative feelings

With this

I'm peeling back the outer layer of my skin

And allowing you to look in

Grope internally

Tour at your leisure

The inner dimensions of my soul's palace and dungeon

Just giving you something to do

In my omission from wherever you are right now existin

You could say my name out loud

And the stars would listen

Because I am your moon

You my sun

We are luminescent

And bring light to night

So that even in darkness

Without you by my side

Just the thought of you

Burns my soul bright

So that I can write

Lyrical Cardiologist

My heart beats with hip-hop and I think in rhyme

My blood pumps with hip-hop

The snare to the bass is how I measure time

My eyes focus with hip-hop

Otherwise this world would be a blur

Lyrical cardiologist I rhyme from the heart

Lyrical archeologist diggin up truth from the start

If I ruled the world

                                    I rhyme/ I spit/ I reflect

I'd free all my sons/ I love em love em baby

                    I've wrote/ it's written/ the meaning's not hidden

Black diamonds and pearls

                    I move/ I decipher/ within this cipher

If I ruled the world

If I ruled the world?

I do rule the world

I rule my world

We rule the world of hip-hop

All aboard on this soul train on tracks above buildings and crops

Cause it's BIGGER than

Brooklyn/ crooklyn/ niggas shook an/ I took in much less at first

    than I really could handle/ then it hit me/ bombin my soul like

    the spray can of a vandal

It's BIGGER than

The 4 track/ the 64 track/ the Cadillac/ oh he's wack/ what we lack/ is connection/ lyrics as an armor serve as protection/ cause it won't stop/ till we get the fakeness off the block/ gotta roll together another 365 on this intergalactic rock

It's BIGGER than

My fly Mecca shirt/ these fly timbs/ my boy's 20 inch rims/ lyrics like an extension of my limbs/ spit like whims/ spontaneous/ oblivious/ to bein unjust/ not self-righteous/ everything's right just spittin from the heart

It's BIGGER than

Booty shake/ I want this earth to quake beneath my lyrics/ enormous spirit/ Godzilla/ nothin realer than when I spit/ you spit/ we all spit/ you all get it/ and let it in/ set rhythm/ of words to the break beat/ like my Adidas hit concrete/ rock solid/ sedentary/ mentally aimed and ready/ steady/ aim/ fire/ BOOM!

It's BIGGER than me

It's BIGGER than we

It's gonna be

It's gotta be

So see/ and hear it here

Hip from my left ventricle

Hop to my right

I rearranged my cornea now these words are insight:

Some lace themselves in Ecko/ Mecca/ and Wu-wear/ their discmans feeding them lyrics into the center of the ear/ they hold dear their icons who grace Vibe and The Source/ feenin for platinum/ or driving Navis down the same course/ defend their favorites with no remorse/ spittin' in cipher after cipher till they get hoarse/ weed and Henny a fuel to many/ but I don't need that shit/ I don't need that shit/ I don't need that shit/ cause if I'm thirsty the lyrics will get me bent/ and if I'm hungry the bass line will keep me fed/ ya'll don't know what's materializing within my head/ but my brain serves as my pencil and paper when I'm lacking lead/ these rhymes take me through my high times and low/ like a river on the track of ebb and flow/ nice and smooth/ sometimes I rhyme slow/ sometimes I rhyme quick/ but I need these words cause they're a perfect fit/ to my god-given frame/ and my mother-given name/ I'm not reachin for fame/ but these riffs ain't a hobby/ or an avocation/ when lost on my path they pinpoint my location

YOU ARE HERE

in mind/ body/ spirit/ and soul/ give me your hands so I can let you take hold of the track/ you may lack the bass/ but we'll find your snare/ enter this hip-hop to see where/ I begin and hope to end/ ahead on this journey/ spoken through many mouths but all in the voice of me/ me the triumphant/ me the gritty/ me the loved/ me the city/ me of hope and grace/ and class and taste/

and hips and lips/ and moves that groove/ the beat the rhythm/ of what I give 'em/ to the tune/ the pitch/ with perfection/ and no glitch/ there's no hitch/ it's a ride/ and you're welcome inside/ to take the tracks through the tunnels of my consciousness/ I grew up on this/ these words of culture and mind/ written on lines/ laid down on tape/ let's get high of the beat ya'll

escape

Don't Get It Twisted

DON'T GET IT TWISTED

I wear name brands but I know who I am

And think style is something every person should understand

As not confining but how you're refining yourself

It doesn't matter what clothes you pull off the shelf

Walking the path of life

Is just like strolling the catwalk

With the sun as your spotlight you're rolling for delf

DON'T GET IT TWISTED

The bandwagon drove by and I missed it

I've enlisted in this lyrical army of spoken word kamikazes

Who sacrifice our souls when we filter them through ink onto
    pressed trees

To cease minds

And synchronize their time with mine

Sometimes three minutes just ain't enough to get out every line

DON'T GET IT TWISTED

I like makin the lil' change here and there

But I spit to make ya'll get out your chair

To open minds and make heads aware

To find out where I'm at and take ya'll there

Money is the root of all evil so I steer clear

Of those whose words share the same soil

They ain't tryin to till and toil

They be bloomin now but they're just annual/ I'm perennial

DON'T GET IT TWISTED

I wear booty shorts and tight pants

I love to dance

But don't test my soldier stance

I can back that ass up to knock down anyone attempting to prance

Through my fortress and this kingdom

Wisdom ain't determined by the height of my heals

If you catch yourself knockin my boots sayin I ain't real

Try clickin yours together to get you back over the rainbow

Here's some food for thought for your first home cooked meal

DON'T GET IT TWISTED

I'm young but I'm bright

I ain't afraid to be wrong

But I'm often right

I listen to hip-hop before I go to bed every night

Nodding my head as I sleep tight

I plan to be world wide like excite

www.Amandadiva.com

My brain is a full throttle search engine for what's true and what's
    just a mask being put on

DON'T GET IT TWISTED

Just cause you got locks

Don't mean a perm is fake

Men love to say what's beautiful bout women

But don't know how much we have to take

Daily just to continue to be ourselves and live carefree

Since elementary girls feel like Pac "All Eyes On Me"

Cause whatever you do to feel pretty

If it's buyin hair or getting your nails done weekly

Is only petty

If what's beneath the surface ain't worth a penny

DON'T GET IT TWISTED

I don't want your man

Cause I shook his hand

Or complimented his lyrical command

Understand that type of thinking

Is like swollen glands

The predecessor to sickness

So catch it/ get some antibiotics

Envy is infectious and attacks more then just each organ

I don't want those germs so I'll be careful not to shake your hand

DON'T

DON'T

DON'T GET IT TWISTED

I've come into the game

And I'm gonna remix it

I'm not writin bout revolution yet

Cause I'm still fightin my own battles

I can't pick up a gun

If I'm still holdin a rattle

Young fresh and clean

At twenty I'm ready to be seen

As more than just a girl

But a queen

And in jeans or a mini

Spittin for free or a quick fifty

I'm always comin with full soul intensity

No holdin back

If you think I don't know bout the talking that goes on behind my
back

That cause my shirt may be buttoned low you wonder if it's
morals I lack

Then you have got it twisted jack

I'm well read and only seek to learn more

Hollarin FEED ME/ FEED ME

Like Kasim or Seymour

I'm light years ahead

Warp speed in my next generation

Me and the right track are running adjacent

You need to be facin the mirror

So you can see your picture clearer

Cause one thing that keeps me nearer to the Almighty

Is I know how he made me

And unless your hands hold his divinity

Keep them in your pockets

My spirit needs no adjusting

You can't change me

My Mother

~for Nets

My mother

Annette Ingrid Seales

Of Grenadian birth

Speaks with an accent

And seasons my dreams with jerk

My hopes with nutmeg

And my wishes with saffron and curry

A 5'8" Amazon

Full-blooded West Indian

She made sure I knew where my roots were sunk

Since day one

A hero unsung

I sing her song

The Caribbean melody that forever rung throughout the rooms of
my home

And the ears of my American mind

Infiltrating my speech with plantain sweetness

She may be a U.S. citizen

But within her veins runs the blood of Carib and Arowak Indians

So when I speak of my mother

My linguistics start *ta* smell of *acki and sal' fish*

Bakes and rum cake

Ox tail/ boneless chicken roti/ and pepper stake

I equate *de* love of my Caribbean culture *wit* my mother

Who was more than just a mother

She was a *brotha*

A *fatha*

And gave me *everyting*

From me last name

To *ma* fresh *mout'*

Born in L.A.

At eight we relocated to de south

A self-sufficient

Independent

Single-mother like no other

She smothered me in

Bob Marley/ Sparrow/ Sade/ Anita Baker/ Elton John/ and
  Stevie

Mr. Rodgers/ Zoobilee Zoo/ and Sesame Street

8 o'clock on Thursdays was Cosby

And I *cyan't* forget birthday parties at Chucky Cheese

Everybody *tanks* God for their success

But I *tank* him for blessing me with Annette

Who *work* two jobs all my life so *we ain't haf'* to live in no projects

Who broke her back to have me in tap/ ballet/ ice-skating/
  piano/ violin/ and gymnastics

Packin lunches for thirteen years

Wipin my tears

Runnin my bath

Makin me laugh

Dance lessons in *de* living room

It took me a while to *whine* me waist on beat

But *Nettie* always kept me in tune

She's more *dan* just my personal maternal being

She's *ma* eyes when I'm not seeing

De truths and realities that are over my head reeling

She's my beacon *ta* shore

When *de* next point on course I'm not sure

Guiding me through *de* dark

She's my night-light

I mean I don't understand how someone human could always be
   right?!

My mother watchin me jump on *de* trampoline

My mother takin me *ta* lessons *ta* learn how *ta* sing

My mother singing songs and never knowing *de* words

My mother makin me Bird's Eye custard

My mother who had me reading by age two

My mother who when I say, "Holla back youngin" answers
   "whoo whoo"

She's far from perfect

But *cyan't* get any closer *ta* being angelic

Praised me when I did good

And when I wasn't I got one set *a licks*!

I used *ta* cry and scream and shout but now I thank her all *de* time

For never being sub par but always being sublime

My mother is words that rhyme

Complimenting my last line

Makes it possible for *de* next thought to incline

And take me closer *ta* my dreams that she marinates in *jerk*

My hopes that she dashes with *nutmeg*

And my wishes that she simmers in *saffron* and *curry*

I learned from a queen how to rule over my own kingdom

Swallowing with spoonfuls of jell-o her wisdom

I catch myself saying quotes

Mimickin her actions

Saying words like she does

And having identical reactions

And where others dread their moms and the day that they become her

I don't have that fear cause I know that I could never ever be as fly as my mother

Lady Like

I am constantly being told how to be lady like

By those whose genitalia looks nothing like mine

Funny how men feel privy to telling me under what conduct I
should abide

I don't hide behind femininity

Craving for somebody to label me sexy to try to sex me

That is of no importance to me and my daily routine

Of being myself no matter what situation I am put in

Boys and men alike

Need to take a hike down a different path than the one I'm trekkin

If they have the nerve to give me instructions on how I should be
actin

Reacting with amazement if I extend my hand to give a pound

Complaining that that is not a gesture that should be found in a
lady's body language

I should extend my hand slightly

So he can squeeze it lightly

That might be how you feel

But I'm unconcerned with how you view my sex appeal

Full of zeal and feminine essence naturally embedded in my
presence

You best except my pound or dap as a show of love and
understand its relevance

Cause at this point in my life I know what type of woman I am
and hope to be

And whether I shake your hand

Give you a hug

Dap you

Or give you a kiss on the cheek

I'm still the same being with a womb and ability for seeing

Truths and realities that you might not even realize are over your
head reeling

True story:

I was once told by a young man that dealing cards made a female
look hard

Claimin girls look like they have a penis when they're deciding on
what to discard

My regards to your mother/ cause maybe you need to talk to her

And tell her of the observations on which you refer

Cause I'm sure

That she'll school you on the thoughts you speak

And inform you that your insecurity on women as strength
bearing makes you seem weak

My ace shouldn't offend you

Nor my desire to wear a fitted cap to the back

I don't sleep in a negligee

R and B is not my favorite music I much prefer rap

I call my tattoo a "tatt"

Use words like "nigga"/ "aight"/ and can recognize when
another woman is P-H-A-T/ PHAT

I know where I'm at

But you're busy tryin to place me

In a space more comfortable for your male identity

I'm not your average girl in a video

So don't even attempt at labeling me a hoe

I don't pose

I exist

Feminine by my own standards

I make no apologies if they are not on the list

Of the woman you are looking for

I'm true to this point of view from my surface to my core

I'll chose a pair of Gap jeans any day before Christian Dior

I don't make my face up cause that would be a lie

On my natural skin tone and features do I rely

My third eye yields no mascara

And sometimes/ yes/ my elbows do get dry like the Sahara

But that makes me human

And that's the type of woman I am

Not tryin to appeal to the eyes of any man

Unless I do so for myself first

I'm blessed with self-knowledge anything else would be a curse

Wearin a thong just cause its revered in a song?!

You've got the wrong one

Instead of blinding you with diamonds

I'd rather my inner luminescence shine like that of the sun

A woman raised me to be the woman I am

To give a firm grasp when I shake anyone's hand

I go to the beach and ain't afraid of the sand

I feel closer to God on my feet so when I pray I stand

My power is rooted in estrogen

My grace exudes from within

And I'm proud of my melanin shaded skin

I am Mother Nature's daughter

And Nefertiti's kin

And I'm a Diva

A Queen

And a Lady

No matter **what** situation you find me in

I'm only 19 but my mind is old.-Mobb Deep

Wise Mind

Hot SHIT

I wanted to write some hot **SHIT**

Some blow off the rooftop **SHIT**

Some get you in your gut

Take uninspired writers out their rut **SHIT**

Some makes doubting cats say, "Yooo B, shorty could spit" **SHIT**

Some crazy/ insane

My sharp wit dissects pieces of your brain and displays them on
the operating table of this stage **SHIT**

Some wagin war **SHIT**

Make you go to your shoebox and get your gun **SHIT**

Some bring Assata out of exile

Black Panthers got crooked politicians walkin single file

Rile and rally up the troops

From domino games/ corner stores/ and stoops **SHIT**

Some put down your cell phone

Get off your two way

And connect to this lyrical fiber optic **SHIT**

Some "daaaammmmn a brotha need to start makin some plans
SHIT"

Some "daaaammmmn a sista need to get with the program **SHIT**"

Some pick up a newspaper and read it **SHIT**

Some pick up a drum and beat it **SHIT**

Some find the hungry souls and with this food for thought feed
  them **SHIT**

I took my pen in my hand
And felt the blood circulate the mental command
From my neurological land
To the fingers that spanned my writing implement
And that **SHIT** I was determined to write it

I was insistent on writing some
  Needs to be split into volumes broken down and explained section
                                by section encyclopedic **SHIT**
                                Some the blueprint for life
                                Building blocks of beings
                  Double helix/ deoxyribonucleic acid **SHIT**
                  Some the future needs to hear and see this
So they freeze my words in time to be brought back as the reviving
                  breath of the rhyme cryogenic **SHIT**
            Some cure those coughin up bull **SHIT** with my lyrical
                                Triamenic DM **SHIT**
            Some removing the cataracts off of third eyes **SHIT**
                  Some writing the words of the wise **SHIT**
      Some Nikki Giovanni/ Langston Hughes/ Bessie Smith/
Malcolm X/ Mandela/ Sojourner Truth/ "Ain't I a woman"/
                  strong/ Black and West Indian **SHIT**

Some GO TELL IT ON THE MOUNTAIN
OVER THE HILLS AND EVERYWHERE
That we won't quit
Cause we can't quit **SHIT**
We're a part of hip-hop
So we you know we tick tock and don't stop **SHIT**

But then I realized **SHIT!**

I can only write what I know and how I feel it
And every time I step on stage I'm comin fully equipped to deliver
that hot **SHIT**
Cause this is the only way I know how to live
To use words that rhyme
To sign my name in the heavens
Declaring my creative independence
You see Diva's the descendent of Pharoahs
My heart circulates the blood of slaves
When I spit Chaka Zulu gets hype in his grave
Cause we are warriors
With the hearts of kings
When I write
Wings spread from the lead's script
And my imagination flies across white skies with blue lines

49

And at these times I realize it ain't about writing some

Gimme straight tens

Put a thirty down by name

"Yo, they feelin me, they feelin me"/ **SHIT**

CAUSE THIS IS POETRY!

And I

Like my words

Am only perfect in the eye of the Most High

But I write/ cause if I don't/ I'll probably die

And this **SHIT** that though slick I call **SHIT**/ fertilizes minds

It plants seeds in the heads who don't read the times

These words can shatter glass/ bend steal/ and splinter pine

Now that's what you call some powerful **SHIT**!

I was focused

Blacked out something serious

Totin a loaded #2 plastic plated .22 with a lead filled clip

And I was ready to rip

Feelin like, "Yo, if I don't write some hot **SHIT**, heads wouldn't take notice"

But then I realized…**EVERYTHING I WRITE IS HOT SHIT.**

If it sparks the mind of at least one who hears it

And its truth creates a stink in this perfect rosy world we've been
taught to believe that in we exist

You see I wanted to write some hot **SHIT**

But this is what I came up with

Cause my soul/ spirit/ and inner fire is blazing/ always lit

And everything I write comes directly from it

The Educated Black Man

This piece was inspired by a date I went on with someone I met at the NuYorican Poet's Café. All that I say here, he said himself. Unfortunately nothing is fabricated or even exaggerated. I still chuckle at the ridiculousness of his opinions and arrogance. I invite you to laugh with me.

I am an educated Black man

In my nice car

And Eddie Bauer pants

My hands in my pockets and chest pushed out stance

I buy women drinks

I don't dance

I am an educated Black man

So I can fall in love with any woman

Whether White/ Spanish/ Asian/ or tan

I'm a college graduate so diversity I understand

I am an educated Black man

Brought myself out of the projects and have spanned the globe

From Queens

To Manhattan

Delaware to Maryland

Knowledge of culture is at my demand

So you must be the one with the lacking of sense

A penny for your thoughts but mine are worth at least 25 cents

I'll take you to the movies but know that from whence the featured presentation begins

There need be silence

That is until I again find interest in hearing myself find yet another clever way to ask a clever question

Like what was your first impression of me

Did I forget to mention I am from the Rockaway Projects in Queens

And I **graduated from college** by my own means

I never aspired to play in the NBA

Or be a rap star

I have only sought education and it will serve me best by far

I don't need to spar

My wit has a thousand pounds of punch

I don't eat fast food

I'd prefer a salad for lunch

I'm an educated Black man

The woman I'm looking for can't be bland

But must be funny and intelligent

With a feminine presence

And most importantly respects me and her body

We could do sit ups together

Hold my feet and I'll hold yours

Maximizing our muscle mass together is so romantic

Because I am a Black man and *educated* at that

I can recognize what is high quality and what is wack

That includes Nas/ Jay-Z/ Cash Money and no I'm not done

The least valuable player in the National Basketball Association in
my opinion is Iverson

Neither of the above could take me when push came to shove

So I have no problem giving them no love whatsoever

Talent is something I feel they endeavor to behold

But through my studies I have realized that their gifts are nothing
but fool's gold

Just to be sure

Did you catch that metaphor

Because you're only 19 and I am 24

So there are times when what I say might go over your head

Knowledge from a book that you just haven't yet read

But that's okay because I'll school you on everything you need to
know to be high class

Not high strung and when I say, "go"

Go

You need not trouble yourself with disagreeing with me

Because when you know as much as I do

You're always right/ so no discussion need be

I have a minor in philosophy not only an *educated Black man* I am a
thinker

It's part of my degree

So I will over and under analyze everything you say

Till I have picked your brain enough to not have to eat for the rest
of the day

I will ask you to pay/ just to hear your response

I'm such a kidder

I'm just joking/ making you pay would be the wrong thing for an
educated man like myself to do

Because along with learning

I became a gentleman too

So I'll race to the door with the same speed that I'll race to tell you
how much I read

And I'll pick up the pace on describing the type of woman I need

If you are lagging behind just follow my lead

I want a rose to water so I'm praying you're not a weed

By the way

Do you go to church

What's your religious affiliation

Spirituality is not really Christianity

You use words like space/ aura/ positive/ and negative energy

And I can't think of the proper word but that "Fatey Thing"/
right?

Well I guess that's just your way of being

But I am much more interested in seeing my face in the rearview
mirror while you describe these thoughts

Chuckling to myself on how drunk I was when I met you off of
151 shots

You're hot but not what I'm looking for

You use slang

And will open your own door

Have an opinion different than mine

And though/ like I said/ you're fine

You're just not fun

Because you don't let me believe I'm better than the p.j.'s where I
grew up

And guys who say what's up

And ride the bus

And only have diplomas from the alternative high schools no less

When I do tips I make the proper calculations while they just
guess

I mean damn I need my back patted everyday for not taking a
short cut

But taking the long way to the top

For keeping my hair neatly cropped/ edged/ and tapered

No braids/ or doo-rags

Or bumps at my neck's nape or

Anything but the finest brands

And lotion on my hands

So when I lightly squeeze yours you clearly understand

That I am more than just anyone with a brain and permanent tan

*I AM AN **EDUCATED** BLACK MAN*

The Good Nigga Poem

It is impossible for me to say "NIGGAS AIN'T SHIT!"

And really/ truly/ mean it

Now of course from time to time

You run into that brotha who gives you a weak line

Or that cat that though fine has nothing behind his eyes or
between his ears

Brain lackin

Damn he's probably packin

But c'mon now I can't even play myself

So you say, "NIGGAS AIN'T SHIT!"

Out of frustration for the one that's facin ya

Sayin "Girl let me get your 2way number"

There's a slew of brothas

Who fine as they wanna be

Ain't got a job

Or common sense worth a penny

Spittin bout getting the block on lock

One brotha even told me that I care too much about hip-hop

And needed to give Sisqo his props

Cause he's hot

ARE YOU SERIOUS?!

In this situation you can't help but find yourself saying

Something to the effect of, "NIGGAS AIN'T SHIT!"

I must admit it's hard to have standards cause it makes the
  pickings less
You prayin for the lord to bless you with someone worth a chance
Who cares more about your mind than what's in your pants
But circumstance makes thoughts of romance not even a choice
Cause you're tired of bein mislead by a beautiful face/ fine
  chocolate body/ or smooth voice
But I can't front
I like nothing other
Than a strong/ beautiful/ intelligent/ motivated/ Black brotha
And as many times as female poets come on stage
To discount and denounce you full of rage
I for one always believe and see from this point of view
That for every 10 wack niggas there's got to be at least one that's
  true
There *are* brothas who open doors
Who have seen the East and West coast shores
Who expect more
Than just a fat ass or large breasts
Who take stock in your character and are willing to invest
Who make moves for reasons other than makin a dollar
Who say words like Ma/ Son/ Peace/ One/ and Holla
But know the words of Malcolm/ the Bible/ the Quran/ Gil Scott
  Heron/ Nikki/ and Mandela
Won't sell ya a bullshit line

When asked whose world it is respond, "It's mine/ it's mine/ it's mine"

There are cats who show up on time

Who have never committed crime

And if they have/ did their time and are tryin to climb

The success ladder like all of us

Brothas who ain't self righteous

Who want a strong woman to appreciate

Who don't depreciate but get better the more you learn about them

And want to know all they can about you

Respect your point of view

Wants you to chill with him and his crew

Cause he likes having you around

Not because you can cook

Or clean

Or write his paper for class

Or give him some ass

Or have a hook up to get the fattest sack

He likes having you there because you share the same wave-length

And move to the same rhythm

He gives you a lot and thanks you for all that you give him

There are brothas out there who are like this

I'm lucky to know a few

They don't have a problem with having female friends

Or giving me a pound like I'm a dude

They respect me as Amanda Diva and make me a believer

So as malcontented as I may seem

I can never Black out *all* brothas and not shed light on those that gleam

I may say "NIGGAS AIN'T SHIT!"

But I never really mean it

Cause the minute I start to believe that

What will succeed is

A race of men lost to the constant anticipation of their being lackluster

No need to muster up any sense for change

When your women treat you as though you're estranged

Now don't get me wrong there are those who don't deserve respect

But there are many who possess intellect

They break the mold and make this poem relevant

I love being a Black woman

Cause I have full and total rights to the Black man

And though we get on your backs

One thing you must understand

Is it's just cause we love you and expect only the best

From the link to all of life across this globe from north to south/ east to west

I catch myself saying in dismay "NIGGAS AIN'T SHIT!"

But it never sticks

And dissolves into yesterday

Cause I believe in my brothas

Love your soul and your brown skin

So for those of you who apply to this poem

I thank you for being the men you are but please

Hook up with the niggas who really *ain't shit* and teach them
somethin

The World We Live In

We are the third planet from the sun
Home to water and humans
We garner four types of precipitation
Earthquakes shake nations
Tornadoes uproot
Floods overtake
Mother nature does not fake
Natural disasters are a givin
But there's more to be fearin in this
My friends

The world we live in

I'm a college student
Pay my tuition
Get loans and scholarships to learn
Yet a friend of mine's brother just got out of prison
And is told he can't get financial aid
To get a degree so he can get paid/ legally
Cause the government of Florida
Is no longer giving funds
To those who've served time
Then wonder why they go back to guns

The education system is only open to those who've never fucked
   up
So the same cats gonna keep fuckin up
The same stores are still gonna get stuck up
The same boys and men still getting locked up
Cause school ain't an option unless brothas want to learn how to
   drive a bus
A situation many brothas are facin
That needs alteration that ain't comin no time soon
Somethin that's become a givin in this
My friends

The world we live in

I was discussin with some old friends
The issue of the this "war" we're in
I was curious about their point of view
One remained silent
The other felt it was necessary
The third said we had to retaliate in violence so America didn't
   look like "pussies"!
I said, "You can't garner peace from disruption of peace"
He said, "That's what they did"
I said, "But everyday America is responsible for the killing of
   women and kids"

It may not be with bombs or gas

Or troops with rifles or tear gas

But we deal our hand out sparingly

And take back whenever we chose

America's gotten used to being on top

The untouchable United State of amber waves of grain and cash
crops

When the World Trade Center dropped

The rest of the world did not stop

9/11 was our alarm clock

To say America wake up!

Every great kingdom or nation

From Egypt/ to Rome/ Greece/ and Elizabethan England

Was attacked and beaten

History regards them as fallen

We may be the most powerful now

But that can and has been tested

It's so easy to say we have to strike back to avoid a counter attack

But that's a logical way of thinking

And there ain't nothing logical about war

Life as we know it is being shaken from the core

Here

My friends

In this

The world we live in

A world where Mumia is still in prison
For a crime he had no involvement in
Where the NY state government thinks we should cut a billion
dollars from education
Yet they want to build the Yankees a new stadium

The world we live in

Where ain't nothing holy bout most these Catholic priests
Just that they're looking for a hole to thrust their falsehood in to
make their "sinful" horniness cease
Where R. Kelly don't see nothing wrong with bumpin and grindin
Or apparently statutory rapin
You best believe you can fly
Cause I've seen the tape and this time from the law you won't be
escapin

The world we live in

Where word is bond
A Black man in NY
Has a better chance of catching AIDS than a cab
And most of the ones

Passing em by

By passing judgement

Are being profiled by our own government for being Arab

Where athletes are paid more than teachers

Where congregations can't trust their preachers

Where it took 3 decades and change for Denzel to win an Oscar
   for best actor

And Halle had to take her clothes off to win for best actress

Where Pac and Biggie are dead

Kids still ain't getting fed

Can do the Harlem shake but can't read

Every other brother over 23 seems to have a seed

I stay tryin to understand the ways and means

To figure out how to change it

To let this light of mine gleam

But I am just a poet

Merely a woman with a pen

I get mad frustrated when I rhyme

Cause I don't know how to make the bull shit end

But I'm here tryin to do more than survive

I want to thrive

So I keep my eyes on the prize

Cause a plan I'm gonna devise

My friends

On altering the state of this crazy

Fucked up

Inconsistent

World we live in

Must See T.V.

Far from lackadaisical

This is no time for resting

Some watch the reception contented

I think the dial needs adjusting

The television needs dusting

It seems

But it doesn't really matter cause the screen gleams

With skin tones bright enough to see through the haze

I guess blackness on prime time was just a phase

Where did they all go?

When's the last time you watched a Black "Must See T.V." show

I know Sanford and Son aren't on the run

And the Huxtable's are not struggling

But when you see a Black bus driver on Friends

And a Black waitress on Seinfeld

You think the only way they're gonna get seen is by smuggling

Them in quiet behind the peacock's back

The actors are getting the flack

But they lack

The stories to tell and be told

Of being Black/ beautiful/ and bold

The game is to be sold

But I ain't buyin

And some folks have the nerve to say, "Well, then you should just
    watch UPN"
If that's my only option
Then I'll turn the tube off and pick up my pen
And write something beautiful/ real/ and true
Something with pride that's powerful
Something rooted in reality
Full of the drama/ tragedy/ and comedy of what it means to be
Brown/ dark and lovely
Something from the past
About the future
But steeped in present relevance
Something truly like the Black experience

I Keep Running

~for DJB

I keep running

Pushin

Pullin

Writhing

Twisting

Tuggin

With every inch of my soul

Every millimeter of my spirit

Every ounce of my blood

To get out of love but it just won't let me go

I walk around believing I'm rid of its grasp

Thinking to myself

FREE AT LAST

FREE AT LAST

THANK GOD ALMIGHTY

I'M FREE AT LAST

But when I least expect

I find my strength inept

Atrophied is my apathy

And I'm back to being held captively

By that shit   that has no stench

That hurt   that has no antibiotic

Love sick

                    And uninsured

        To date there is still no cure

I   move   with   no   boundary

                        Then am hurled

Back within the realm of being overwhelmed

Feelings becoming a cancer to logic

I forget the present negatives

Enveloped in thoughts nostalgic

All this because I'm still a prisoner

Captive in my own kingdom

Hoping the key to escape

Is the lessons learned and new wisdom

It's them times you smile to keep from

crying

Hug to keep from

falling

Speak to keep from

choking on your heart in your throat

I realize that though I thought I crossed the moat

                          I'm still locked inside

Tongue tied

Hands held behind

If I thought I was exonerated I was just lying

To myself to protect my health

When I catch myself running

Pushin

Pullin

Writhing

Twisting

Tuggin

With every inch of my soul

Every millimeter of my spirit

Every ounce of my blood

I know it's that thing called

LOVE

Cause I'm like a winged bird

Flying with velocity

Beyond stratospheres

Through sound barriers

At warp speed…until you walk in

And I suddenly fall prey to gravity

I'm rooted to a love that holds me hostage consistently

Until I find another love

To open my heart and set me free

Yesterday/ Today/ and Tomorrow

~for "The Prototype"

On days like today tomorrow seems ever so uncertain

Because yesterday I bore the ease of loving you

Yet today I carry your distance's burden

Tomorrow I'll be hurting

Next week I wonder if I'll be

To you/ a love no less but in stasis/ a memory

In a month will I be a time you cherish

And drift to when taking long flights

And indulge in when you're alone

At your keyboard writing till the wee hours of the night

In a year will I be the one that got away

The perfect match you disassembled

The dime you exchanged for ten pennies

The hand you lost in the gamble

On days like today I wonder what tomorrow I'll be

To you who yesterday was still trying to love me

But tomorrow will move one step further from me

To rejoin the confines of your well constructed reality

For me/ today feels like no other day since I've come to love you

Because it's the start of a thousand tomorrows

Of us as yesterdays

And me relearning how to live without you

The Bullshit Fast

I wish I could go on a fast from something other than food

Perhaps/ a bullshit fast

I will for one week vow to not consume or intake any bullshit

In the hopes that at the end of my brief b.s.-less stint

I will be trimmed of at least one pound of it

Damn/ if that was even a possibility

Or held even a glint of hope in this reality

I would definitely make an effort to do so

If it were possible

I would take a trip to Barnes and Noble

And pick a book up just to do it correctly

But the fact of the matter is though I try to do it daily

Resist/ cease/ and desist the bullshit others bring me

It can be a feat rooted in amazing difficulty

Cause it is produced so prolifically

And exuded profusely

I used to be one to take in what was given

And let it effect how I was livin

But those days are gone

I've moved on from that space and time

Cause I'm on a crusade to evade the bullshit whether I'm on the street/ in class/ in my mother's house/ or on stage spittin in rhyme

But even I'm unable to dodge all that comes my way

I believe the only perimeters within which one could truly/truly/ truly

Let every piece of mess/ feces/ and mental waste pass without relay

Would be if we all lived in a fundamentalist state

Where by call of law and religion all inhabitants had to partake

In the fast from sun up to sun down all day/every day

Because there is just too much in circulation

They could sell gourmet b.s. at D'Agastino's or

Two for one at C Town on 150th and Broadway

With how much is produced daily in this nation

And I'll be the first to admit

There is no explanation

For getting caught up in the constant defecation

But the fact of the matter is you can't avoid it cause it's bred from ignorance

And just like inmates in our prisons are always on the rise

It seems like it shares the same rate of elevation

It's found everywhere

So intense that after a conversation lacking sense it's like I can smell it in my hair

The only way I see to divide up the quotient of cacophonous thought

Noise to my head

Trash that is routinely fed

Is to multiply intelligence among other things

Like tact/ humility/ civility/ and compassion

Knowledge is power

So why is it that sometimes I can't propel without fail

When I'm ailed with a barrier of bull

That stands compelled to stop my attempts to excel

Cause well/ sometimes you get caught off guard

Off kilter

Off balance

Or off beat

And you have to stop

Recognize what it is halting you

And then set to planning defeat

I've been met head on

By heads on the same crap I'm speakin on

I know ya'll have too

Some of you may be a part of the demographic I'm alluding to

But I can't take no more shit

From brothas or sistas

Or anyone comin with it

Cause it ain't fertilizing this soil

I'm bloomin just fine with a little sun and a lot of experience

But I digress

It's the thought process

That's where the solution rests

In the minds of those who don't think before they cause distress

Talking bout they have to confess

Professing their ability to analyze minds so want to give me tests

The cure to the bull shit epidemic manifests

In this simple bit of knowledge I've deduced through my quest

To rid my self of the pollutionary element of b.s.

Two lines for your mind that I'm sure you will agree on with no
contest

> That if people would think more
>
> Their minds would shit less

Say it with me if you agree

> If people would think more
>
> Their minds would shit less

So the next time you find yourself in a situation

That looks like it may take the bull shit formation

Repeat those two lines in your mind and keep it movin

We can't be fillin our bodies with that crap when there is
information with nutritional value that we need to be
consuming

Anger Management 101

~For...you know who you are

This is for every soul who tried with all their might to take mine

Punching me with fists of fakeness and stabbing me with daggers
of doubt

Hoping my heart of gold would flat line

Parasites feeding on my insight

Attempting to steal the power of my inner light

Dull/ so they want a piece of me to make em feel bright

Claimin to be big dawgs but their bark's all they got for a bite

Thought they were in the ring with someone unwilling to fight

Till my warrior strength surfaced and had them running in fright

I'm writing this for every person that took my friendship

Knowing they couldn't give it back

Thieves in the night hiding behind masks

Cloaks of kindness covering their hearts of shade

Loyal/ I would've swam the seven seas for them

But they left me in puddles of disappointment to wade

Swallowing seeds of my selflessness but having no nourishment
for me

Feeding me empty promises seasoned with indignity

This is for the many who looked me dead in the eye and lied

Each time reaching in and burning my insides

This is for the one I believed in with every inch of my spirit

And told him time and time and time again just to make sure that he could hear it

The one who told me he believed

The one who called me the one

The one who predicted and so I wished it that one day we'd have a daughter and son

The one who stopped loving me because he realized he wasn't sure what love was

The one who had me crying in silence on the train and on the bus

The one who when I tried to break the ties to the pain came running begging to hold on

The one who wouldn't let me not be his friend because he said he couldn't live with me gone

The one who when lost I came to his rescue

The one who when sick I prayed for everyday

The one who when cured didn't even remember those words

And has yet to visit me to this day

Who taught me the reality of living in a dream

And the nightmare when you realize things aren't as perfect as they seem

This is for the one who almost made me give up hope

Who made me turn to poetry just so I could cope

This poem is for all those who did their damndest to break down
    my protective barrier
Only to reveal themselves as wackness carriers
Beings polluting the waters of my good nature
With frustration/ disappointment/ and hatred
This is for the losers
The fronters
The forsakers
The liars
The confused
The doubters
The takers
The haters
For all those who could've broken my spirit and stride
But through these words I keep the rhythm alive

You snakes and serpents who violated my trust
Who infected me with your incompetence through every
    insufficient thrust
Who filched me of respect because you hated yourself too much to
    treat me with it
Who don't deserve the air you breathe because you're so damn
    unappreciative
Who toyed with my emotions and played with mind
Then went on with your life leaving me behind

This poem/ unlike you/ is solid and sincere and real and true

And for the times you took my smile and gave me a frown

Along with it I have two words that are all yours

FUCK YOU!!!!!!!!!!!

NAScent Poet

~For the emcee who keeps me thinking

Contradiction on his diction bears no weight

On his infliction of rhythm and activism into the realm of the
rhyme

Through verbal intercourse he rapes tracks

With syllabic thrusts raw and unstrapped

Every groove of each truth digging deep

Hittin your gut

Bending your mind back/ over/

And beyond the bullshit

My nigga spits

Goddamn my nigga spits

I've gone hoarse in his defense

My vocal strength strained

Relaying the reality of his street colloquial claims

To those who negate his skill and question his aims

I show no shame/ exhibit requisite respect

For his descript and illicit dialect

Breakin my neck/ expanding minds

My nigga can rhyme

All praises to Allah my nigga can rhyme

Many fashion their understanding of his revolutionary style
Against the antithetical profile of the industry and while
They fluster and fidget about what to do with it
Where to place it amongst the crooks and thieves
Bloods and Crips
Gangstas and consciousness
It exists within its own nucleus
Cellular structure non-descript
Cause it's the best secret
But you can peep it/ the illness
It's frequent in filled spaces between the lines
In each joint's unique design
In how his words fire like a glock
Over the beat that knocks

My nigga can rock
Word up/ my nigga can rock

Beats/ Rhymes/ Life

Ears ringing with the sounds of the beat
Sounds like stompin concrete
Or poundin lunch tables
Or beatin on trash cans after school
    to pass the time till tomorrow

Looks like the streets outside
Movin fast and slow by my bus window
Changin pace with the seasons
Slow in summer
Quick in the cold

Feels like the earth moving
Or the tide coming in
Chaotic focus
Easy/ intense
Like the moment before you feel the thrust of a love movement

From what I know of them, funerals usually garner sad words and melancholy metaphors of life and death. I do not know much about funerals, but I did know Sonia Noriega and that she would want nothing do with that. This is for her. We miss you.

A Poem for Sonia

Sonia cherished the 80's as if it were still '87

Madonna and George Michael hits all day will be her heaven

Petite but unaffecting her spirit and soul

I'm sure that/ like she did on earth/ beyond those pearly gates she
    will take control

Breaking molds as usual she'll abandon a halo and wings

For a tee shirt/ jeans/ and some Doc Martins

I met her on a Saturday that seems like yesterday

Unpacking her things in a dorm room 5000 miles away from her
    beloved L.A.

I called her Son-i-a

Because she was definitely a sister to Californ-i-a

A valley girl myself we'd pay homage to the mall

She lived two doors down the hall/ and we made use of our close
    location

Writing papers on the phone/ while we made corrections

I'd be done in two hours/ but Noreaga searching for perfection

Would wake up needing confection for she'd had 3 hours of sleep

"I thought I was done-but then I wasn't" is how she'd explain it to
me

Then we'd walk to breakfast to get cornbread muffins and coffee

And discuss our latest annoyances with the acting company

Sonia had savory sarcasm so thick it melted on your tongue

With wit she kept our classmates hung/ on the edge of each
comment

Sent poems to me when boys were causing my mind problems

Sonia always advised on how to solve them "Amanda he doesn't
deserve you"

True blue/ with red arms after early mornings of yoga

Drinking soda/ and talking with her hands

The quizzical face when things and people she didn't understand

Unafraid to make clear-cut demands

Us Purchase girls brought *life* to P.F. Chang's

She is alive though her body is gone

It's cliché/ but her memory lives on

In so many who had the joy of her friendship

The blessing of her laughter

The comfort of her presence just watching and critiquing the
Oscars

So beautiful/ and strong/ and proud

Of her apartment/ her family/ her talent/ her principles

Her ability to pack efficiently/ her freedom of living independently

Her friends/ her heritage/ her intensity

An individual with her own identity

When we last spoke I told her to "Make it happen"

That things would continue to fall into place because they were
meant to be

This is a blessing from Sonia to all of us who hold her memory

To realize the true transience of our lives

And to see clearly

How much every day matters

And each minute counts

One thing Sonia would want is for us not to frown

It's hard to smile but it comes with ease

With the slight wind of a breeze

That echoes the sound of her laughter in the rustling of leaves

She's a part of our lives

We live knowing there is another pair of eyes

Making sure the paths we tread are safe

And that time we do not waste

She was more than just an actress or a waitress

She was my friend and confidant

A passionate artist

A fire starter

In the immortal words of Sting/ an 80's musical king

Everything she did was magic

And though her death was devastating and tragic

Let it illuminate your minds

Into cherishing time

For life is so short

And people like Sonia are very hard to find

I love her so much

And will keep her with me always

Sonia Isabel Noriega 1980-2001

I swear I've been here before.-Me

OLD SOUL

All I Hold

If I composed a rhyme or prose

Comprised of all I hold in my soul

It would drop like bombs on your minds

Swellin melons with my creative createne

I'd have everyone walkin out the building with a lean

Cause it would take more strength than I could muster

More gusto than I could gather to flow

To deliver the sum whole

Of the contents of my soul

See it's old and heavy

But it's weight keeps me steady

Sittin solid on my heals

Diva Seales the one brothas cock their heads at like

"Yo, this chick is for real"

My zeal is funneled directly

Through a tunnel that connects the

Core of me

To the brain in my cranial cavity

Within those walls exists

A laboratory like that of a mad scientist

Where thoughts connect electric with emotion

Givin powerful current to my flow and

I plug the mic's cord into my afro then

Amplify what I signify

My mind's eye stays dilated

Cause it's got so much to behold

Takin in truths to be told

It converts things seen

Into muscular proteins

That strengthen my being

So I can bust through and break molds

I'm a woman never satiated if not movin

I need this pen

Cause through it

I break the truth down like crazy legs

Never beg/ just bum rush the mind and get mine

Then I spit it onto 32 blue lines

When I rhyme/ I dig deep into my inner sanctum

Reach beyond my epidermis

Navigate through systems nervous

I write the new shit

None can say "Ay, yo, I heard this"

My verses get em hype in New York

Amped in L.A.

Open em in Ethiopia

Awaken em in Asia

Have em buckin from Jamaica to Grenada

Spectators ask for a pause

A break

A breather

When I deliver

Just a portion of the diva

No loose leaf piece of pine

Nor singular self no matter how strong their spine

Could handle the brunt force that would course through my pen

If I allowed ya'll to see EVERYTHING that's in here sittin

On my chest

Strengthenin my back

Remindin me I'm Black

Holdin my id intact

When my ego thinks its fly and makes me forget how to act

Pullin me down to earth

Conquerin my fears

Respectin my elders

But believing in the power of me and my peers

Nah if I let ya'll peer into every recess of my inner atmoshpere

Your mind would explode from its mental contractions

So don't be askin me to get deeper

Or think I'm shallow cause I go by the name of Diva

You'd need a mask and scuba gear to peer into my interior

Not callin none of ya'll inferior

But I'm wide spread like the barrier reef

So suspend your disbelief

I come from suburban summers and gum speckled concrete

Osiris and Isis

And Ossie and Ruby Dee

I love intensely

I live immensely

Always keeping visible this world around me

Through this life I've taken in

Through my ears/ eyes/ and skin

So much sometimes I feel like I can't take anymore in

Full to the brim

Up to my chin

If I put it all into a poem

The weight of the words would pummel your face in

Its velocity would mimic that of a mac ten

A piece so potent

It'd probably bust my esophagus right open as I'm quotin
    Giovanni

Or maybe its energy would dismember me

As I move my arms with the intensity of singing like Mary

Scary to think what it would do

As it pulsated through

My throat/ vocal chords/ and larynx

Spittin lyrics of Nas/ Public Enemy/ Gil Scott Heron/ and Rakim

After I'm done

I probably won't be able to cough or ahem

Cause this soul holds so much in it

The past/ future/ and present

I need this poetry

Just to keep from spontaneously combustin

So I bust my ass

Bustin these rhymes

But I can only give ya'll a lil bit at a time

Cause if I gave you everything upon which my soul was defined

I might as well just learn how to sign

Cause I'd have nothing left to say

41 Shots

41 SHOTS CAN'T HOLD ME DOWN
4 JAKES CAN'T KEEP ME ON THE GROUND
WILLIE LYNCH CAN'T SILENCE MY SOUND
JIM CROW CAN'T STEAL MY CROWN
I RISE LIKE THE SUN AND SHINE LIKE ONE AND SHINE LIKE ONE
I RISE LIKE THE SUN AND SHINE LIKE ONE AND SHINE LIKE ONE

I knew rivers/ built pyramids then they housed me in tenements

Crowded me on ships used whips the Atlantic held no sentiments

Warrior strength the brink of insanity lay at my feet

Tread gingerly duality exists in this identity

Many years my peers and elders were welders and pickin

Cotton/ layin steel/ working in fields where hatred's unhidden

Unseen as citizens/ they're choppin cane

Stolen/ hopin for better than what remains

Lord/ it's so hard to ease the pain

The world on my back like Atlas holdin the weight of many

Link to life on earth since man's birth now they sell me for pennies

So I chop the auction block into wood/ burn and press it into
    paper

Thrust my pen in ink and script on how to escape the

Trappings of this United State/ where they tried to control my fate

Put on front lines to fight a fight that wasn't my fight to fight/ I
    need strength

For the plight of gaining my rights/ tired from watchin strange
    fruit swingin

Eyes stinging

Trying to keep focus on the prize and hear freedom ringing

They want me to put my drum down and stand still

But I've got the blues/ and I'm spiritual so I'm singing

41 SHOTS CAN'T HOLD ME DOWN

4 JAKES CAN'T KEEP ME ON THE GROUND

WILLIE LYNCH CAN'T SILENCE MY SOUND

JIM CROW CAN'T STEAL MY CROWN

I RISE LIKE THE SUN AND SHINE LIKE ONE AND SHINE LIKE ONE

I RISE LIKE THE SUN AND SHINE LIKE ONE AND SHINE LIKE ONE

You know me/ the one bearing melanin coming from the sun

Zulu nation growing impatient with waitin for my time to come

So I rise/ realize/ take matters into my own hands

World War I done to Harlem we comin fleein from Southern
    lands

Renaissance of artisans/ creatin/ writin on my people

Culture equal though society acts violently and their hate is lethal

But I'm resilient/ resistant to bein held down

They try to steal my beauty/ box me in and destroy my crown

Impossible I move and groove to rhythms unstoppable

Have a dream to move racial mountains and make 'em topple

Was born from kings/ stolen but never broken called dumb and
  ignorant
Couldn't describe my vibrance dubbed me colored
Changed to Negro then
I took back my power
Black is beauty
Though some believe different
Now a citizen combining cultures call me African American
My history untold it's in the earth and the stars
The first human on this planet I'll be the first to visit Mars
Blasting from my speakers as I'm intergalactically cruising
Can't nobody take my shine
Can't nobody hold me down
Oh no I've got to keep on movin cause

41 SHOTS CAN'T HOLD ME DOWN
4 JAKES CAN'T KEEP ME ON THE GROUND
WILLIE LYNCH CAN'T SLENCE MY SOUND
JIM CROW CAN'T STEAL MY CROWN
I RISE LIKE THE SUN AND SHINE LIKE ONE AND SHINE
  LIKE ONE
I RISE LIKE THE SUN AND SHINE LIKE ONE AND SHINE
  LIKE ONE

Black is surviving slavery/ marching through Montgomery/ Selma and D.C.

Riots in Watts and L.A. on t.v.

Black is panthers with power ammunition for revolution

Tried shootin discrimination out of this nation/ to get racism uprooted

Black is Malcolm/ Martin/ Louis/ Stevie/ Jessie/ W.E.B.

Ella/ Maya/ Rosa/ Aretha/ Angela/ Fanny/ Nikki

Black is the '68 Olympics/ fists in the air to fight

The NAACP helping bring light making futures bright

Black is kids getting in fights/ on corners all hours of the night

Slingin rocks/ projects/ totin techs/ for death not having fright

Black is passing as white to make life a little breezier

Denying culture in the hopes that life would be a little easier

Black is powerful/ ashy elbows/ collard greens and grits

Jerk chicken and peas and rice

Mos Def on both sides

Cross colors and Cazalles

132 and Lenox

Black is Carver Shores/ Tangelo Park/ Pine Hills/ and Paramour in Orlando/ Florida

Black is the blues

Black is jazz

Black is the cha cha slide

Black is hip-hop

Black is bloods and crips/ afros and lips/ guns and knives/
    husbands and wives

From Brooklyn to Compton/ Black is different to each set of eyes

Black is many shades and shapes/ hair/ music/ and identities

Black is beautiful

Black is ugly

Black is free

Black is me

And I say it loud

I'm Black and I'm proud cause

41 SHOTS CAN'T HOLD ME DOWN

4 JAKES CAN'T KEEP ME ON THE GROUND

WILLIE LYNCH CAN'T SILENCE MY SOUND

JIM CROW CAN'T STEAL MY CROWN

WE RISE LIKE THE SUN AND SHINE LIKE ONE
    AND SHINE LIKEONE

WE RISE LIKE THE SUN AND SHINE LIKE ONE
    AND SHINE LIKE ONE

Sometimes I Wonder

Sometimes I wonder why I do this shit

Why I bother to spit

Why I get on trains to do shows all out in Hempstead

In a room with only like 22 heads

Why I carry my rhyme book

And always a pen

Just in case I get moved to write another poem

Why I never leave with out a cd up in my purse

Why I spit in the shower and the mirror to rehearse

Why I'm up at 2:30 am cause I'm on a roll

Why I'll truck to the Nuyorican no matter the rain or the cold

Why I go to all these venues

Why I spit at all these spots

Why I grind on the grind no matter how it takes up time

Why I listen so I can give em' some shit that's hot

Why I keep on keepin on with the politics of these poetics

Ain't no record deals or endorsements like those in athletics

Why I run these streets like calisthenics

Just to roc a mic

Why it matters so much that I get a crowd hype

Sometimes I wonder and then I realize

After I step off the stage and look into the eyes of somebody
    moved by my poetry

Or who like it enough to buy a cd

Sometimes I get blinded by "divaness" but humbleness let's me see

That I keep doin this cause though the struggle's bigger than me

These words are my revolution

They're my own piece of the movement and when others can see the vision I see

Or feel the glory that I'm persuin

It makes it all worthwhile

I Think I Bleed Ink

I think I bleed ink

Cause when I'm hurt I see Black/ or blue/ or red

The hurt I feel felt by words on lines being read

Spread my thoughts across the paper

Emotions seep across my lips

Keep a pen behind my ear so I'm always fully equipped

To script the rage in my veins

Divert sanity to sane

I range from poet to poet with lessons learned in between

Maintain a steady flow of mind movements

If I think it

I'll do it

Doubt me

And I'll prove it

The sky's the limit

And I pursue it

To galaxies beyond/ I pen my points

So when I'm gone the school kids'll read my joints

And see that this art turned inner pain to inner peace

My heart pumps with hip-hop my mind eases with the beat

Invisible Man

Sometimes I feel like a fatherless child

Sewing his oats he didn't imagine that they'd go wild

And beguile him into the life-long responsibility that is a child

That is a daughter

That is his blood

That is me

The one and only first-born

Unadorned with praise and support

God-forbid I get less than straight A's on my report card

This from a man who pardoned himself from raising me

14 days out of 365 is nothing more than government forced
   paternity

Due to his distance I grew aware from an early age

That in my book of life I did not want him to have a page

But that wasn't up to me the words were already written

From the day my mother made the phone call to tell him

That after years of infertility specialists

And believing she'd never get the chance to bear

Or carry for nine months a seed that would grow with her care

She was blessed with a miracle and blessing that astounded

The doctors were confounded

Yet my father found it

A burden that unto him a child would be born

My mother with a back of granite and a womb of steel

Of self affirmed middle class and rejection of all things genteel

Born of island suns and hurricanes

Verandahs and colored windowpanes

Refusing to feign her excitement

That unto her a child would be born and she would not fight it

"It might not fit into your life plans but I will make it essential to
    mine

If you can find time to raise this child then do so at your leisure

This it, will become a woman and neither of us need ya"

Nine months later among stirrups and white walls

Tiled corridors and gurney speckled fluorescent-lit halls

Bearing scrubs and a need for inclusion my X chromosome

Came out from hiding to see my entrance into this world riding

The waves of my Mother's hopes

And bearing the sands of my his fear

Twenty years later his actions to this date are still unclear

A graduate of Tuft's and an M.D. from Harvard this man

If ignorance were his alibi then perhaps I could understand

Why he was never there to hold my hand when I crossed the street

Or why I couldn't open my birthday presents because I didn't eat
    my vegetables

I'd understand

Why calls were only necessary on holidays

Why I wasn't special enough for just everydays

Yet my Mother calls me everyday from 3000 miles away

While he resides across a bridge in New Jersey!

All that used to unnerve me until I realized

It's his loss if he wants no part of me

"Daddy where have you been" is no longer a question emblazoned on my mind

He's six-feet tall but I've been the bigger person since I was four foot nine

There was a time when he was an ever-present nemesis

That plagued me like a growing mental cyst

Filled with so much anger and hate that it created an orifice in my simple place of bliss

But I refuse to repeatedly react to the fact that when it comes to child rearing he is simply remiss

When I'm on television stations

He'll be trying the hardest to get reception

Bragging about his seed that he nurtured with rejection

When I look in the mirror it's his features that are in the reflection

Yet my strength is my mother's and my last name is hers as well

His presence in my life *he's* taken the initiative to quell

I refuse to be the chip on my shoulder's lackey

So I choose to be happy because I am

The child

The blood

The daughter

The result of my mother

And what her mother taught her

My father is merely an invisible man

Unresponsive to the human

That though he created and wasn't part of the plan

Will stampede this globe when he's deceased

Full of fire/ through words my visions are released

My power is ever present and everlasting is my inner peace

And with or without him in my life it will never cease

I thank him for giving me life

Cause it takes two to create one

But sometimes I wonder

Would things have been the same had I been a son

My Sole

My soul is like the Brooklyn Bridge
Constantly under construction
Rooted in the same soil
But the sunlight stays fluxin
So my leaves change
And my flowers bloom when they are of the notion to
Running on my path I keep changing my shoes

I used to tread in heals uncomfortable and unsure
Watching my step
Not knowing if the road was safe
Or if I could endure
Should I be demure
How can I be more than cute
It's time to retire the one-piece bathing suit/ right?
Looking in the mirror not pleased with what was before me
Cause it didn't look womanly…more like elementary
So I wore those heals at home when no one was around
Wishing my feet were bigger
To fill the shoes that I found
But those toes were round
And mine point straight ahead
So if the clouds block the stars

Or the birds eat all the bread

I'll know the way to the ginger bread house and won't get stuck
with a shed

But I was led down a different path to something else

Wishing the boys liked me

Wishing my pants fit tightly

Even changed my facial expression so that as I walked around I
smiled slightly

Cause maybe that was more welcoming than gliding through the
day in thought

A furled brow I fought

As my posture remained taut

My head caught up

I finally realized I had to slip those off

Only to try on another to make the walk less rough

My skin tough from the cramped quarters of attempted grace

I found my place in shoes with rubber soles and ties to lace

But I continued to face the mirror

Now less elevated

But of a higher learning

Young mind and body always yearning

No sterling silver spoon

Mine was stainless steel

And I fed myself distress trying so hard to appeal

To the eyes and ears of others

My perspective shared by no sisters or brothers

My cushioned soles made it easy to walk behind foes

Searching for friends that on I could depend

That with time I could spend

So I shouldn't have to fend for me/ myself and I

But even my arch was supported

Liquid gel enhanced

Ankle supported sneakers couldn't keep them from passing me by

My best friend had to end our relationship

Cause I didn't pluck my eyebrows and never painted my lips

She was fully equipped

But I was not of the same reflection

My tenth grade homecoming dress was found in the kids section

She made me vex and hurt all at the same time

Thought I was keepin up

But I was still behind

And in those days I didn't think to rhyme to get it out

Or had the ability to sing instead of to shout

Wanting so bad to gain clout

But not aware of what that was about

It was a minute before my route shifted and the sands sifted

Removing the stones in my path as I was lifted

North of my youthful residence

To dormitory tenements

Tuition and meal plans

For me the least important elements

Cause my vents were inhaling a new breath of air

Now out of my Nikes I wore long/ tall/ high / Black boots

And was fully aware

Of any man's stare

Or any woman's glare

That I had "good" hair

And a sexy flair

Willing to share my positive attitude

But still/ what was I trying to exude

And what for

Cause as long as I keep welcoming others in they're just gon' keep
closing the door

Before I wanted to be grown

Then I wanted to be fly

Prone to gaining approval

Now I wanted to be me but kept getting asked why

I act the way I do

And say the things I say

And, "who are you to call yourself Amanda D-I-V-A"

I had no answer that back to the inquisitors I could relay

So elevated in my boots from my roots and beginnings

I was playing games with myself while folks watched me struggle
   through the extra innings
Sending slings and arrows across my path
I couldn't dodge them easily
The weight of the boots lessoned my agility
My reality was a fallacy
My "me" was someone else that I was trying to be

Finally my back sore and feet over worked
I unzipped the boots and found where the problem lurked
Not under my skirt
Or between my thighs
Or in my toes
It was behind my eyes
Cause the prize I was shooting for was already in my possession
And though I have a great gpa
That's got to be my greatest lesson learned
I've got to be me not those others I yearned for
And though I get curious at times and pry those shoes out from
   under my bed
They stay in their boxes cause I like my bare feet instead
They ain't perfect
And my nail polish chips
And when the road gets slick
I sometimes slip

But it's the feeling of the ground against my skin

That reminds me of what race I'm in

And when I get slowed

How to begin again

I ain't tryin to win no praises anymore

Or work hard for others just to make my muscles sore

There's a lot in store

And I can't afford any leg cramps

Due to wearin shoes that make my feet cramped

My stride is easy flowing I'm going with where the wind moves
me

Not weighed down by emotions that didn't move me

I'm free to point/ flex and extend my soul and spirit to wherever it
can reach

Fully aware that though I've gained knowledge there's still more
for this world to teach

And my soul's under construction daily

But I don't need steel toe boots

No objects will be falling that can cause me harm

Cause now I only bare the fruits of my labor

And they're ripening daily

The shoe doesn't fit anymore cause I only need the strength of the
sole God gave me

Reminiscin on Tommorrow

As I bob my head
The feet of the future and the past tread
Up and down the sidewalks lined with buildings instead of trees
These communities of youth and elderly
Though gapped by generation
Come together face to face
In the music in my soul and headphones

The break beats of yesteryear
The downbeats of tomorrow
Syncopatin the happiness of today
Or tonight's sorrow
Is borrowed boldness now giving color
To what some deemed a bleak horizon

The times have changed
But the melodies remain
Wrapped now in Gucci and red gold chains
But on the train
I write to unlink them with status
And reconnect them with truth
To rest on the graves of the soon gone
And on the fingertips of the youth

This Pencil

Sometimes I feel like I can't write
Because there's just too much to say
As if words would validate the chaos that's within my head
Expression at times is easier said than done
There are moments when my pen feels like the weight of my spirit
At least a ton
It's those times when my center burns like the sun
When my woven world of sanity seems undone
The rhythm of my cursive
Of lead against blue lines
Brings me back
Regaining the togetherness I spontaneously lack
No more a damsel in distress
I get off the tracks
This pencil brings me back
When I've lost sight of fiction or fact
The reflection of me isn't so exact
It re-assembles my contents and gets me intact
I've got fast twitch emotions so I'm quick to react
This pencil brings me back
These lines of symmetry
The consistency of collecting my self into words

Is ritual in itself

A ceremony of sanctifying my faith in me
By illustrating the page with this vocabulary
                                    When my voice gets tired
I write so that I can see my thoughts more clearly

When I Die

3/23/00

revised 12/23/01

When I die, I want to be wearing pink. From head to toe. And everyone who walks by me as I rest in eternal slumber, clutching a copy of Shange's *For Colored Girls Who Have Considered Suicide When the Rainbow is Enuf,* will say, "Damn, she even matched at her funeral."

When I die, it *will* be that deep. Because I will die with the understanding that my identity was within. It was not how different or crazy I was. It was a sense of place. It's a way of knowing I'm not a rock or that tree. I'm this living creature over here. I am part of my surroundings and I become separate from them. Because you don't know what you're giving if you don't know what you have, and you don't know what you're taking if you don't know what's yours and what's somebody else's. [1] Your identity lies in the finding of the God within yourself and loving her fiercely.

When I die I hope no one who ever hurt me cries, and if they cry, I hope their eyes fall out and a million maggots that had made up their brains crawl from the empty holes and devour the flesh that

---

[1] "It was a sense of place…" Excerpt from Anne Deveare Smith's, *Fire's in the Mirror*

covered the evil that passed itself off as a person I probably tried to love.[2]

When I die I don't want invitations to be sent out. Those who truly loved me and recognized my spirit will know the moment they open their eyes that very morning that I'm gone. And will inquire themselves as to why the sun is missing a ray of light today.

When I die, I want all who felt it worth their time on earth to come and pay their respects to my time spent on earth, to look each other in the eyes and without even being described in some long drawn out eulogy, probably delivered by each member of my close circle of friends in verses like the Wu, to be able to know and understand that Amanda was real. That ten times Amanda, equaled Amanda multiplied next to one. It was all the same, and it was all genuine. All the energy, all the laughs, all the dancing, all the sarcasm, all the hugs and kisses on the cheek, all the love punches reserved only for my dawgs, all the pink, all the weakness for beautiful black men playing basketball in the sun, all the hip hop, all of the clothes and shoes, all of the hair, all of the respect for her Grenadian roots, all of the big ups to the dirty south, all the pictures, all the blunt statements, the doodling on my hand out of boredom, and all the love I had for everyone who had proved themselves non injurious to the joy of my kingdom, was REAL. Not manufactured or fake, but 100% pure. And those who knew that, received it, and will keep it forever.

---

[2] "When I die..." Excerpt from Nikki Giovanni's, "When I Die"

I would be lying to say I am not afraid of dying. Yet, I am not afraid of living. I live my life with compassion, and with everything that the Lord gives me. I grow at the rate I'm supposed to grow, and know that I won't miss the boat. I'll always be right on time.

When I die, I want the sun to be shining, and **everyone** in pink. I want them to sing Sting's "Every little thing she does is magic", and blare Nas's "Who's World is This" through the treetops. To serve cranberry juice and cornbread muffins, my favorites. But most importantly, I want them to dance. Everyone needs to dance; to revel in the fact that while I was here, I was as true to myself and to them as the grass they're dancing on is green. And as they dance barefoot to the sound of my body lowering in the ground, and Lauryn Hill blaring, "Ooh-la-la-la it's the way that she rocked when she was doin' her thing", a slight sun shower will wash the tears off of my mom's face, sprinkle the permed hair of all my girlfriends from college, and fog the glasses of my ever sophisticated friends who for once don't stop what their doing to polish their lenses, but instead stay dancing. And this little drizzle of summer will let them know that I will always be there, waiting in the clouds, thundering with energy, and beaming as bright as the sun, with laughter and love.

It's bigger than hip-hop. Remember that.

About the Author

In the summer of 2001 Amanda Diva burst onto the poetry scene as a spoken word emcee whose style, an energetic blend of hiphop and Black history, humor and intensity, strength and intelligence, stood out from the now exploding poetry scene. "Diva Deev" has blessed mics from Russell Simmons' Def Poetry Jam (2002), venues all over the tri-state area, and the stages of college campuses across the U.S. Continuing to spread the rhyme she has served as the face of hip-hop for Mtv2 and you can currently hear her rockin the airwaves every morning on Sirius Satellite Radio's, "Hip-hop Nation". Her vocals can also be found on her own Spoken Word/ Soul cds, "It's Bigger than Hip-hop, The Mixtape: Vol.1" and "Never a Dull Moment" (www.AmandaDiva.com). She is a recent graduate of Columbia University with a Masters in African American Studies.

Printed in the United States
29147LVS00006B/1-111

9 781418 436896